THE POWER OF GOAL SETTING

A master life skill for achieving great success

Includes 75 classic quotes on goals

Gabriel Aryeetey

LIFE AND SUCCESS PUBLISHING
www.abookinsideyou.com

Copyright © October 2011 Gabriel Aryeetey All rights reserved.

No part of this publication may be produced, distributed, or transmitted in any form or by any means, including photocopying, recording, or other electronic or mechanical methods, without the prior written permision of the publisher, except in the case of brief quotations embodied in critical reviews and certain other noncommercial uses permitted by copyright law.

For permission requests, write to the publisher, addressed "Attention: Permissions Coordinator" at the email address below:
Life and Success Media Ltd
e-mail: info@abookinsideyou.com
www.abookinsideyou.com

Unless otherwise stated, all scriptural references are taken from the King James Version of the Bible. Other versions cited are NIV, NKJV, AMP and KJV. Quotations marked NIV are taken from the HOLY BIBLE, NEW INTERNATIONAL VERSION. Copyright © 1973, 1978, 1984 by International Bible Society. Used by permission of Hodder and Stoughton Ltd, a member of the Hodder Headline Plc Group. All rights reserved. "NIV" is a registered trademark of International Bible Society. UK trademark number 1448790. Quotations marked KJV are from the Holy Bible, King James Version.

THE POWER OF GOAL SETTING
ISBN: 978-1-907402-88-3
Cover Design: **MIA**Design.com

Author: Gabriel Aryeetey
Telephone: 079836 13544 [UK]
+44 79836 13544 [Outside UK]
Email: peakdestiny@ymail.com

CONTENTS

Introduction [7]

Chapter 1: Take charge of your destiny [9]

Chapter 2: The Relevance of Goals [13]

Chapter 3: Understanding Goals [19]

Chapter 4: The Process for achieving your goals [25]

Chapter 5: Quotes on Goals that ignite, inspire, challenge, build and motivate. [29]

ACKNOWLEDGEMENTS

My deepest and sincerest gratitude to God for introducing me to who I really am in Him and charging me with the great responsibility of working out my purpose He gave to me.

Charles 'Tremendous' Jones was right when he said that you are the same today as you'll be in five years except for two things, the people you associate with and the books you read.

I am incredibly grateful to the various mentors I have learnt from through personal interaction, seminars, books, DVDs, CDs and the internet. I particularly want to acknowledge my spiritual father Dr Michael Hutton-Wood for all his input into my life. You have been such a great role model to me.

My heartfelt gratitude to my parents Rev Ernest Aryeetey and Mrs Hannah Aryeetey for all your love and sacrifice to raise my brothers and I up with godly wisdom.

Last but not the least my fondest gratitude to my darling wife Mrs Yvonne Aryeetey for your love, care and support everyday of our marriage.

INTRODUCTION

The current world population currently stands at 6.93 billion humans. Out of this number many people feel as if they are adrift in the world. They are constantly busy, they work hard at home, on their jobs, but they don't seem to get ahead in life.

I came to discover that one of the key reasons why they feel this way is that they haven't spent enough time thinking and writing down what they want from life; they haven't set themselves formal goals. I however shudder to think that any of us would set out on a major journey with no real idea of our destination.

So why do many people go through life which is major journey with no sense of purpose and direction. My aim in this book is to provoke the reader into taking up this skill of Goal setting.

Goal setting is a powerful process for thinking about your ideal future, and motivating yourself to turn your vision of this future into reality.

The process of goal setting helps you choose exactly what you want to achieve in life and more importantly why you want to achieve it. By knowing exactly what you want to achieve, you begin to discover who, what, how, why, when and where you have to concentrate your efforts. This skill is used by top level athletes, successful entrepreneurs and achievers in all fields of endeavour.

I believe that by the time you finish reading this book you would experience a paradigm shift concerning goals and be on your way to being a high achiever. Let's go.

Chapter 1

Goals 101 - Take Charge Of Your Destiny

'Our deepest fear is not that we are inadequate. Our deepest fear is that we are powerful beyond measure. It is our light, not our darkness that most frightens us. We ask ourselves, who am I to be brilliant, gorgeous, talented, and fabulous? Actually who are you not to be? You are a child of God. Your playing small does not serve the world. There is nothing enlightened about shrinking so that other people won't feel insecure around you. We are meant to shine, as children do. We were born to make manifest the glory of God that is within us. It's not just in some of us; it's in everyone. And as we let our own light shine, we unconsciously give other people the permission to do the same. As we are liberated from our own fear, our presence automatically liberates others.' Nelson Mandela, Inaugural Speech 1994. Originally from Marianne Williamson, A Return to Love.

Life is meant to be lived by design, not by chance.

In the book 'What they don't teach you in the Harvard Business School', the late Mark McCormack tells about a study conducted on students in the 1979 Harvard MBA Program. In that year the students were asked, 'Have you set clear, written goals for your future and made plans to accomplish them?

What was the answer? You may be guessing. Only 3% of the graduates had written goals and plans, 13% had goals, but they were not in writing and a whopping 84% had no specific goals at all.

10 years later, the members of the class were interviewed again, and the findings, while somewhat predictable, were nonetheless astonishing. The 13% of the class who had goals were earning on average twice as much as the 84% who had no goals at all. What about the 3% who had clear written goals and plans to accomplishing them? They were earning on average 10 times as much as the 97% put together.

My dear friends, about 5 years ago I was really hungry to do something very significant with my life. I had this burning desire to be very successful in life. To be named among the 3% most successful and wealthy people you would find in any part of the world. More importantly I just wanted to live with a real purpose in life. I started looking for successful people around me, reading about them, listening to and watching them on TV; I wanted to find clues on how they made it, how they became who they were now especially those from an impoverished background. I wanted to find how they thought, what they practiced behind closed doors and one of the skills I discovered was that they were all goal-setters or visionaries. They always started everything with a goal or a vision in place.

Ladies and Gentlemen, before I really became serious about writing clear specific goals and putting down plans of action to accomplish them, I would probably say I fell within the 13% category of the class.

I inherently had the passion to see myself succeed in anything I did, especially at school. But I hardly ever took a pen and paper or went behind a PC to type out my goals whether short term or long term.

Everything I wanted to achieve at any stage in my life then was all in my head which was very wrong, however through my formal schooling years right up to University level, no teacher ever taught me about goals and the power behind setting goals. Definitely not their fault as the educational system as a whole never had subjects like these in the curriculum. In hindsight, believe me if there was any course or module like Goals 101, Goals 201, I would have taken it.

Most of us have all being through this educational system or similar ones; no wonder a lot of people are meandering through life with no sense of direction and purpose. We are being reactive to life's demands and not being proactive as to what and how we want to design our lives. Do not get me wrong, I applaud our educational system for what it's being able to achieve however I believe it has never really taught us on everyday life skills which is one of the most important ingredients for success in life, family, business, ministry, money and the quality of one's life. As Brian Tracy puts it '**The ability to set goals and make plans for their accomplishment is the "master skill" of success**.

Goal setting has been described as the single most important skill that one could learn and perfect in reaching their peak performance by renowned high achievers all over the world. Goal setting will do more to help you achieve the things you want in life than will anything else you've been exposed to. Becoming an expert at goal setting and goal achieving is something that we absolutely must do if we wish to fulfil our potentials as human beings.

Goals enable us to do the work we want to do, to live where we want to live, to be with the people we enjoy, and to become the kind of person we want to become. And there is no limit to the financial rewards we can obtain. **All we have to do is to set a goal for financial success, make a plan, and then work the plan until you succeed in that area.**

Chapter 2

Goal 201 – The Relevance Of Goals

Discipline is the bridge between goals and accomplishment.

Jim Rohn

What is Goal setting?

Have you ever wondered what goal setting is and what it can do for you? To make it simple, Goal setting is the process of writing down something you want to achieve in your life and working out a plan to achieve the results you desire. Just like a vision which our Creator gives to us, He wants us to immediately write it down. So what can a goal do for you? Think about it, if you desire to be wealthy, and you constantly see your goals, will you remind yourself to take the necessary action to make your goals come true?

Of course you will, and this is what goal setting can do for you. A goal can help you to stay focused in taking action. The moment you see your goals on your desk, you will remind yourself, you will tell your mind that you have a mission to accomplish, and therefore you will be driven to take action.

Nothing happens until you take the necessary action with strategy. That is why goal setting works and people who set goals achieve what they want from setting their goals.

Why only a few people set goals?

The payoff for setting goals and making plans is being able to choose the kind of life we want to live. So why do so few people set goals? According to the best research, less than 3 percent of people across the world have written goals, and less than 1 percent review and rewrite their goals on a daily basis. So the reasons why people don't set goals have been of considerable interest to me. I learnt from renowned personal development leader Brian Tracy that there are five basic reasons why people don't set goals.

The first reason why people don't set goals is that they don't **understand the importance of goals**. 'Nothing is truly yours until you understand, not even your own self'. A majority of the 7 billion people in the world have never understood the significance and the invisible power behind setting goals in life. Right from the beginning the Creator himself was goal oriented. He knew He wanted to create man and the right environment for him by the end of the sixth day so that He could rest on the seventh day. My dear friends there is an invisible power behind us seeing what we want clearly in our minds and hearts and writing it down. Our Creator Himself has put this awesome power behind setting goals.

Habakkuk 2:2 from the great book makes this so clear:

And the Lord answered me, and said, write the vision, and make it plain on tables, that he may run that readeth it. For the vision is yet for an appointed time, but at the end it shall speak, and not lie: though it tarry, wait for it, because it will surely come. It will not tarry.

Proverbs 4:5 and 7 also says:

'Get wisdom, get understanding: forget it not; neither decline from the words of my mouth.

'Wisdom is the principal thing; therefore get wisdom: and with all thy getting get understanding.

We see from the above scriptures how God is passionate about having a vision, a goal written down and worked at to be realised at a specific time which we call deadlines. God explicitly says that the vision or goals we write down will definitely materialise, we will definitely see the physical manifestation. Friends, I beseech you to start developing the skill of setting goals on a daily, weekly, monthly, quarterly, yearly basis and long term goals to design the life you want to have. Find your purpose in life and set goals to achieve everything the Creator meant for you to fulfil on this earth.

The second reason why people don't set goals is because **they don't know how to do it.** One of the greatest tragedies of our educational system is that you can receive 15 to 18 years of education in our schools and never once receive a single hour of instruction on how to set goals. The reason for this is that most of the people who designed the syllabus are not goal oriented themselves. Yet in schools where goal setting programs have been introduced to children at a young age they become excited about goal setting, even if the goal is only to increase their scores by 5 or 10 percent over the course of the term, or to be on time every day in the course of a month. Children become so excited about achieving goals that by the third or fourth year, they love to go to school and get the best grades. They are seldom absent, excited about themselves and about their lives. So encourage your children to set worthwhile and realistic goals from an early age.

The third reason why people don't set goals is **fear of rejection**. The fear of rejection is caused by destructive criticism in early childhood and is manifested in adulthood, in the fear of criticism by others. Many people hold back from setting worthwhile goals because they have found that every time they do set a goal, somebody steps up and tell them that they can't achieve it or that they will lose their money or waste their time, efforts and investment.

Have you ever in been in a situation where you were so excited about a goal, a new direction for your life, dream and went telling people only for them to tell you that you cannot accomplish it, you are living in a dream land, you should be so foolish to think you could ever achieve it or do something that is more than what the average individuals does. Sometimes they would genuinely say it because they have been so used to living mediocre lives.

Because each of us is strongly influenced by the opinions of those around us, one of the first things that you must learn when you begin setting goals is to keep your goals confidential. Don't just tell any 'tom dick and harry' about them. Often, it's the fear of criticism that, more than any other single factor, stops people from goal setting in the first place. So keep your goals to yourself, with one exception. Share your goals only with others who are committed to achieving goals of their own and who really want you to be successful and achieve your goals as well. Even better never be influenced by people's opinions. All you need is the affirmation of your Creator and you and you are already in the majority.

The fourth reason why people don't set goals and perhaps the most important reason of all - is the **fear of failure**. People don't set goals because they are afraid that they might fail. In fact, the fear of failure is the greatest single obstacle to success in adult life. It can hold you more than any other psychological problem.

The primary reason why we fear failure is simply this: We do not understand the role that failure plays in achievement. The fact is that it is impossible to succeed without failing. Failure is an indispensable prerequisite for success. All great success is preceded by great failure. If you wish to fulfil your potential, you have to be willing to risk failure over and over and over, because there is no way you can ever accomplish worthwhile goals until you have fallen on your face so many times that you have eventually learned the lessons that you need for great achievement.

In doing research for his classic book, The Law of Success, Napoleon Hill interviewed more than 500 of the most successful men and women in America. All of them admitted to him that they had achieved their greatest successes just one step beyond the point where they had experienced their greatest failures. A key to succeeding through goal setting is expecting temporary setbacks and obstacles as inevitable parts of the goal-achieving process.

Now, in order to be successful, you need to focus your mental and physical energy in a single direction toward a predetermined objective. People who are especially energetic or talented have a hard time with this. They are the ones who try to do several things at once and end up doing nothing well. Setting well defined goals enables you to channel your efforts and focus your energy toward something that's important to you. Goal setting gives you a target to aim at and enables you to develop the self-discipline to continue working toward your target rather than becoming distracted and going off in other directions.

Chapter 3

Goals 301- Understanding Goals

All successful people, men and women are big dreamers. They imagine what their future could be, ideal in every respect, and then they work every day toward their distant vision, that goal or purpose.

Brian Tracy

Let me share with you five keys that I learnt from Brian Tracy that will help you to reach your goals more effectively. Each of these keys starts with one of the letters in the word goals. Whenever you find yourself getting off the track, simply repeat the word goals, and think about how each letter stands for a key that just might apply to your current situation.

The first letter is G, and it stands for Get to it. Sometimes, the only difference between a successful person and a failure is that the successful person has the courage to get started, to do something, to begin moving toward the accomplishment of a specific goal.

Brian said that when he was younger, he realized that because of his limited education, he was stuck in a low paying job. He began reading the job vacancy section of the newspapers and decided that He wanted to work in advertising, especially as a copywriter. He went to an advertising agency and applied for the job of writing advertisements. The head of the agency was very polite, but told him that he was unskilled and totally unsuited for the position. He thanked him for coming in and wished him luck.

Now he was back on the street, but he had a goal. He wanted to be an advertising copywriter. He immediately took the first step, which was to learn more about how to write copy, so that He would not be turned down in the future because of a lack of ability. He went to the local library and checked out books on the subject of advertising and copywriting. Over the next 12 months, He checked out and read every single book in the library on the subject. Meanwhile, He read magazines and newspapers and thought about how He could improve their advertising. He wrote sample advertisements and began taking them to advertising agencies.

To make a long story short, at the end of the 12 months, two of the largest advertising agencies in the country offered him a job as a copywriter, and He accepted one of those offers. His income doubled. He had worked at other jobs in the meantime. But He had never lost sight of his goal, and he had kept on doing the things that he needed to do to put him in a position to eventually achieve his goal.

You too, may have a long range goal. In order to achieve it, you need to sit down and make a list of all the steps that you will have to take to get from where you are to where you want to be. Then begin with the first and most obvious thing that you can do on that list. Complete it, and then start on number two. Don't worry about the long term. Just concentrate on the obvious first step that you can take. Surprisingly enough, everything else will take care of itself. Remember the Confucian saying, 'A journey of a thousand leagues begins with a single step.'

The second letter O stands for opportunity. Successful people do not wait for opportunities to turn their goals into reality; rather, they create their opportunities, because they are perfectly clear about the kind of life they wish to create. Once you have taken the time to decide exactly what you want, you will experience an endless flow of opportunities that will help move you in that direction.

When I finished university in 2005, I was now about to face the real world. I remember right after my dissertation for my Cost Benefit Analysis module I was scheduled to come over to the United Kingdom. I knew that the UK in itself was not going to determine whether I would be successful or not, I would have to have my own goal or vision of the level of success that I would like to enjoy. I had to create my own future regardless of where I was going to settle down. Right away I had a goal of becoming a great leader in the field of personal and professional development as well as building an entrepreneurial career. My plan was to start reading as many books as I could lay my hands on, CDs, DVDs, attend seminars in these fields of endeavour. I remember buying my first books 'Winning Attitude' by Dr John Maxwell and 'Releasing Your Potential' by Dr Myles Munroe in Ghana. I started reading them right away and continued even harder when I got to the UK. As I write this chapter, I've just ordered the book 'Secrets of the Richest Man that ever lived' by Dr Mike Murdock. The opportunity came for me to be introduced to a great church by my Auntie whom I lived with. The Senior Pastor Dr Michael Hutton-Wood is a spiritual and intellectual genius I can never get tired of listening to his messages or reading his books. Seminars were not left out, I've had countless opportunities to attend seminars all over UK from stock market investing, property investing, seminars organised by my church, preaching engagements with my Bishop. There have been more opportunities to take up leadership positions in church, in business, and I'm definitely on my way of reaching my goal of being financially independent by the age 35.

The letter A stands for ability. Many people hesitate to set high, challenging goals because they think they lack the ability necessary to turn those goals into reality. Never just look at your physical ability and resources to achieve any significant worthwhile goal. Every great accomplishment especially a vision given by our Creator will definitely require supernatural ability as well. Even when it comes to your physical ability, remember when you started your first job? When you first started to learn how to ride that bicycle, you probably felt a little clumsy, inadequate and unsure about how to do it well. As you progressed and got more experienced, you became more and more confident, and in many cases, you did an excellent job without even thinking much about it. Since you gain the ability necessary for high achievement through knowledge and experience, if you increase the speed at which you acquire both of these, you increase the speed at which you move ahead.

The letter L stands for leadership. Leadership is simply the ability to get results. And you begin to get results when you accept full responsibility for yourself and for the outputs required in your position. You demonstrate leadership when you refuse to make excuses or blame anyone or anything for the challenges you are facing. The acceptance of the responsibility of leadership enables you to move ahead and take action. When you are not satisfied with your job or income, and you sit down and make a written plan to change it, and then take action on that plan, without waiting for anyone's approval or permission, you are behaving like a leader.

The final letter, S, stands for stay with it - the resolution to persist in the face of adversity until you succeed. Between you and every goal that you wish to achieve, there is a series of obstacles and the bigger the goal, the bigger the obstacles. Your decision to be, have and do something out of the ordinary entails facing difficulties and challenges that are out of the ordinary as well. Sometimes your greatest asset is simply your ability to stay with it longer than anyone else. When you look around you, you will see that all achievement is the triumph of persistence. You will see men and women everywhere who are struggling with and overcoming adversities in order to accomplish something that is important to them. And so can you.

So these are the words and phrases to remember in setting and achieving goals: The first is get to it! Get started; take the first action at hand. The second is opportunity. Begin to prepare yourself now so that you will be ready for the opportunities that will inevitably arise. The third is ability. Resolve to learn what you need to know to live the kind of life you want to live. The fourth word is leadership. Take charge of your time and your life, and accept responsibility for your results. And, finally, stay with it. If you stay with it long enough, nothing can stop you from finally winning through.

Chapter

Goals 401-the Process For Achieving Your Goals

If you go to work on your goals, your goals will go to work on you. If you go to work on your plan, your plan will go to work on you. Whatever good things we build end up building us

–Jim Rohn

1. **Decide exactly what you want and why you want it:** Before anyone can achieve anything of worth in this life you have to know and decide exactly what you want and why you want it. What exactly do you want in your life and why do you want it?

Because once you can find a reason strong enough the how to achieve it becomes so easy even when you haven't got a clue as to how you are going to achieve it.

I once attended an interview in the city of London and the interviewer asked me a fundamental but very crucial question. He asked, why do you want to have a better life, why do you want to be wealthy? I was trying to be conservative with my answer because I thought that would make him probably change his mind if I sounded too ambitious. I was actually wrong, he wanted to hear more, and he wanted to feel the passion with which I was delivering the answer. He then gave me the example of Thomas Edison who invented electric light. Thomas knew what he wanted to achieve for humanity, he wanted to create a much brighter form of light but didn't know how to go about it initially. People including renowned scientist thought that it was impossible and he had gone mad but Thomas believed in his reason for wanting to have bright light so much so that even when he tried almost 10,000 times and did not get it right he never gave up and eventually discovered the how in achieving his dream.

2. **Write it down**: The good book instructs us to write down our vision and goals so that whoever reads it will run with it, Habakkuk 2:2. It is never enough to just have your goals up in your head. There are mere wishes at this stage. There is a supernatural backing when you write down what you want to achieve in a goals journal, in your PC, I Pad, diary etc. Friend, write it down now!!!

3. **Set a deadline to achieving it**: Goals written down always have to have a measureable defined period for its achievement. This places a demand on our Creator to send all the people, capital, resources and opportunities needed for its realisation. That's why when you set your goal and makes plans to achieve them inevitably opportunities just keep coming your way like it is some magic. No, our Creator himself orchestrates these opportunities for us to take advantage of in reaching our goals. Have specific dates in mind written down to accomplish your goals. I have personally seen so many of my goals that I typed out on my laptop become reality by the dates I assigned to them.

4. **Make a list of everything you are going to do to achieve this goal:** Every goal will require that you will have to take a couple of intentional actions to see it materialise. Whatever your goal is, make a list of the things you need to do to achieve the results you want to see. Whether it's reaching a set financial target, starting that dream business, reducing your weight etc take time to write out every single thing you believe you need to do to achieve your goal even the ones you supposedly think you cannot do.

5. **Turn this list into a plan of action:** From the list of things you wrote down, you would need to devise a plan as to how you want to achieve it. This is simply writing down with a systematic approach the steps you would be taking and when you would complete them. A plan of action helps you to purposefully work towards your goal irrespective of challenges you may face on your way to achieving your goal. If you haven't got an idea as how to achieve your goal look for a mentor who is accomplished in that field of endeavour and be determined to learn from him or her with all humility.

6. **Resolve to do something every single day that moves you forward along that plan**: Decide and strongly determine to do something everyday towards the achievement of your goal even if they are baby steps. Let no day passed by without you working on your goal, your dreams. Spend at least one hour a day working on your goals, dreams. Dr Hutton-Wood once said, 'Success is not in what you do occasionally, success is in what you do habitually.' Every baby step towards your goal or dream is described as success. Mamie McCullough said, **'Success consists of little daily efforts.'**

Chapter 5

Goal 501- Quotes On Goals That Ignite, Inspire, Challenge, Build And Motivate.

1. A goal properly set is halfway reached.

    Zig Ziglar

2. If you want to reach a goal, you must "see the reaching" in your own mind before you actually arrive at your goal.

    Zig Ziglar

3\. People are not lazy. They simply have impotent goals - that is, goals that do not inspire them.

Anthony Robbins

4\. People with clear, written goals,
accomplish far more
in a shorter period of time than people
without them
could ever imagine.

Brian Tracy

5\. Goals allow you to control the direction
of change
in your favour.

Brian Tracy

6. If you go to work on your goals, your goals will go to work on you. If you go to work on your plan, your plan will go to work on you. Whatever good things we build end up building us.

Jim Rohn

7. We are the creative force of our life, and through our own decisions rather than our conditions, if we carefully learn to do certain things, we can accomplish our goals.

Dr Stephen Covey

8. Chase your passion, not your pension.

Denis Waitley

9. Setting goals is the first step in turning the invisible into the visible.

Anthony Robbins

---

10. Goals provide the energy source that powers our lives. One of the best ways we can get the most from the energy we have is to focus it. That is what goals can do for us; concentrate our energy.

Denis Waitley

---

11. There are only two words that will lead you to success. These words are yes and no. Undoubtedly, you've mastered saying yes. So start practising to say no. Your goals depend on it.

Jack Canfield

12. Discipline is the bridge between goals and accomplishment.

Jim Rohn

13. Success is steady progress toward one's personal goals.

Jim Rohn

14. Go confidently in the direction of your dreams. Live the life you have imagined.

Henry David Thoreau

15. Learn from the past, set vivid, detailed goals for the future, and live in the only moment of time over which you have any control: now.

Denis Waitley

---

16. When you are in the valley, keep your goal firmly in view and you will get the renewed energy to continue the climb.

Denis Waitley

---

17. I'm a big believer in growth. Life is not about achievement but learning and growth, and developing the qualities like compassion, patience, perseverance, love and joy and so forth. And so if that is

the case I think our goals should include something which stretches us.

Jack Canfield

---

18. The major reason for setting a goal is for what it makes of you to accomplish it. What it makes of you will always be the far greater value than what you get.

Jim Rohn

---

19. If you raise your children to feel that they can accomplish any goal or task they decide upon, you will have succeeded as a parent and you will have given your children the greatest of all blessings.

Brian Tracy

20. If what you are doing is not moving you towards your goals, then it's moving you away from your goals.

Brian Tracy

---

21. When you know what you want, and want it bad enough, you will find a way to get it.

Jim Rohn

---

22. All successful people men and women are big dreamers. They imagine what their future could be, ideal in every respect, and then they work every day toward their distant vision, that goal or purpose.

Brian Tracy

23. Don't be a time manager, be a priority manager. Cut your major goals into bite-sized pieces. Each small priority or requirement on the way to ultimate goal becomes a mini goal in itself.

Denis Waitley

24. A goal is to get what you see on the inside to happen on the outside.

T D Jakes

25. You can become an even more excellent person by constantly setting higher and higher standards for yourself and then by doing everything possible to live up to those standards.

Brian Tracy

26. The more intensely we feel about an idea or a goal, the more assuredly the idea, buried deep in our subconscious, will direct us along the path to its fulfilment.

Earl Nightingale

---

27. Obstacles are those frightful things you see when you take your eyes off your goal.

Henry Ford

---

28. Goals are dreams with deadlines.

Diana Scharf Hunt

29. The road leading to a goal does not separate you from the destination; it is essentially a part of it.

Charles DeLint

---

30. Success isn't a result of spontaneous combustion. You must set yourself on fire.

Arnold H. Glasow

---

31. Goals are the fuel in the furnace of achievement.

Brian Tracy

32. People with goals succeed because they know where they are going.

Earl Nightingale

---

33. Until input (thought) is linked to a goal (purpose) there can be no intelligent accomplishment.

Paul G. Thomas

---

34. Nothing can stop the man with the right mental attitude from achieving his goal; nothing on earth can help the man with the wrong mental attitude.

Thomas Jefferson

35. The average person with average talent, ambition and education, can outstrip the most brilliant genius in our society, if that person has clear, focused goals.

Brian Tracy

36. By recording your dreams and goals on paper, you set in motion the process of becoming the person you most want to be.

Mark Victor Hansen

37. When the promise is clear, the price gets easy.

Jim Rohn

38. Begin with the end in mind.

Dr Stephen Covey

---

39. Reasons come first.
Answers come second.

Jim Rohn

---

40. Rewrite your major goals every day, in the present tense, exactly as if they already existed.

Brian Tracy

---

41. I will always set a goal and work towards it because even before I finally achieve it, I know I would have been a better person than I was before.

Gabriel Aryeetey

---

42. To solve a problem or to reach a goal, you …. Don't need to know all the answers in advance. But you must have a clear idea of the problem or the goal you want to reach.

W. Clement Stone

---

43. My philosophy of life is that if we make up our minds what we are going to make of our lives, then work hard toward that goal, we never lose- somehow we win out.

Ronald Reagan

44. Our goals are reached through a vehicle of plan, in which we must fervently believe, and upon which we must vigorously act. There is no other route to success.

Stephen A. Brennan

---

45. The establishment of a clear, central purpose or goal in life is the starting point of all success.

Brian Tracy

---

46. Decide what you want, decide what you are willing to exchange for it. Establish your priorities and go to work.

H L Hungt

---

47. We all have two choices. We can make a living or we can design a life.

Jim Rohn

---

48. Crystallise your goals. Make a plan for achieving them and set yourself a deadline. Then, with supreme confidence, determination and disregard for obstacles and other people's criticisms carry out your plan.

Paul Meyer

---

49. To be fully alive a person must have goals and aims that transcend himself.

Herbert A Otto

50. Write it down. Written goals have a way of transforming wishes into wants, can't into cans, dreams into plans, and plans into reality. Don't just think it, ink it.

Author Unknown

---

51. Fear melts when you take action towards a goal you really want.

Robert G Allen

---

52. The victory of success is half won when one gains the habit of setting goals and achieving them. Even the most tedious chore will become endurable as you parade through each day convinced that every task, no matter how menial or

boring, brings you closer to fulfilling your dreams.

Og Mandino

---

53. Leaders are made, they are not born. They are made by hard effort, which is the price all of us must pay to achieve any goal that is worthwhile.

Vince Lombardi

---

54. Take the pains required to become what you want to become, or you might end up becoming something you'd rather not be. That is also a daily discipline and worth considering.

Donald Trump

55. The big secret in life is that there is no big secret. Whatever your goal, you can get there if you're willing to work.

Oprah Winfrey

---

56. Peace is not merely a distant goal that we seek, but a means by which we arrive at that goal.

Martin Luther King Jr.

---

57. When we are motivated by goals that have deep meaning, by dreams that need completion, by pure love that needs expressing, then we truly live life.

Greg Anderson

58. Without goals and plans to reach them, you are like a ship that has set sail with no destination.

Fitzhugh Dodson

---

59. I feel that the most important step in any major accomplishment is setting a specific goal. This enables you to keep your mind focused on your goal and off the many obstacles that will arise when you're striving to do your best.

Kurt Thomas

---

60. Life's ups and downs provide windows of opportunity to determine your values and goals. Think of using all

obstacles as stepping stones to build the life that you want.

Marsha Sinetar

---

61. Never look down to test the ground before taking your next step, only he who keeps his eye fixed on the far horizon will find his right road.

Dag Hammarsjold

---

62. If you are bored with life, you don't get up every morning with a burning desire to do things, you don't have enough goals.

Lou Holtz

63. If one advances confidently in the direction of his dreams and endeavours to live the life which he has imagined, he will meet with a success unexpected in common hours.

Henry David Thoreau

64. The trouble with not having a goal is that you can spend your life running up and down the field and never score.

Bill Copeland

65. Goals are not only absolutely to motivate us. They are essential to really keep us alive.

Robert H. Schuller

66. If you have a goal in life that takes a lot of energy, that requires a lot of work, that incurs a great deal of interest and that is a challenge to you, you will always look forward to waking up to see what the new day brings.

Susan Polis Schultz

---

67. The tragedy of life doesn't lie in not reaching your goal. The tragedy lies in having no goals to reach.

Benjamin Mays

---

68. Progress has little to do with speed, but much to do with direction.

Author Unknown

69. The world makes way for the man who knows where he is going.

Ralph Waldo Emerson

---

70. When you determine what you want, you have made the most important decision in your life. You have to know what you want in order to attain it.

Douglas Lurton

---

71. Set your goals high, and don't stop till you get there.

Bo Jackson

72. Success is the progressive realisation of a worthy goal or ideal.

Earl Nightingale

---

73. Do it now. You become successful the moment you start moving toward a worthwhile goal.

Author Unknown

74. By losing your goal, you have lost your way.

Friedrich Nietzsche

75. The greatest thing in this world is not so much where we are, but in what direction we are moving.

Oliver Wendell Holmes

Peak Destiny

Gabriel Aryeetey Is The Ceo And Founder Of Peak Destiny.

Peak Destiny is a personal and professional development company in the business of training and developing individuals and organisations to discover and maximise their visionary and creative endowments to reach their full potential.

If you, your organisation, college, university, business or ministry would like to invite Gabriel Aryeetey for a motivational speaking or training engagement including increasing productivity from your staff, increasing sales revenue from your sales executives you can contact us on 079836 13544 [UK] +44 79836 13544 [Outside UK] or by email at gabbiebest@yahoo.co.uk or peakdestiny@ymail.com

www.ingramcontent.com/pod-product-compliance
Lightning Source LLC
Chambersburg PA
CBHW071322080526
44587CB00018B/3323